Introduction, Theme and Variations

FOR Bb CLARINET AND PIANO

Gioachino Rossini

Edited by David Glazer
Piano arrangement by Ralph Hermann

OXFORD UNIVERSITY PRESS
NEW YORK • OXFORD

Introduction, Theme and Variations

for B♭ Clarinet and Piano

Piano arrangement by
Ralph Hermann

GIOACHINO ROSSINI
Edited by David Glazer

This edition may be played with band accompaniment arranged by Ralph Hermann.

VAR. 1

VAR. 2

Introduction, Theme and Variations

SOLO Bb CLARINET

GIOACHINO ROSSINI
Edited by David Glazer

* See Piano part for original notation.

2

SOLO Bb CLARINET

VAR. 1
Più mosso ($\quad$ = 108)

VAR. 2

VAR. 3
Poco più mosso (♩= 120)

Minore
Largo (♪= 64)

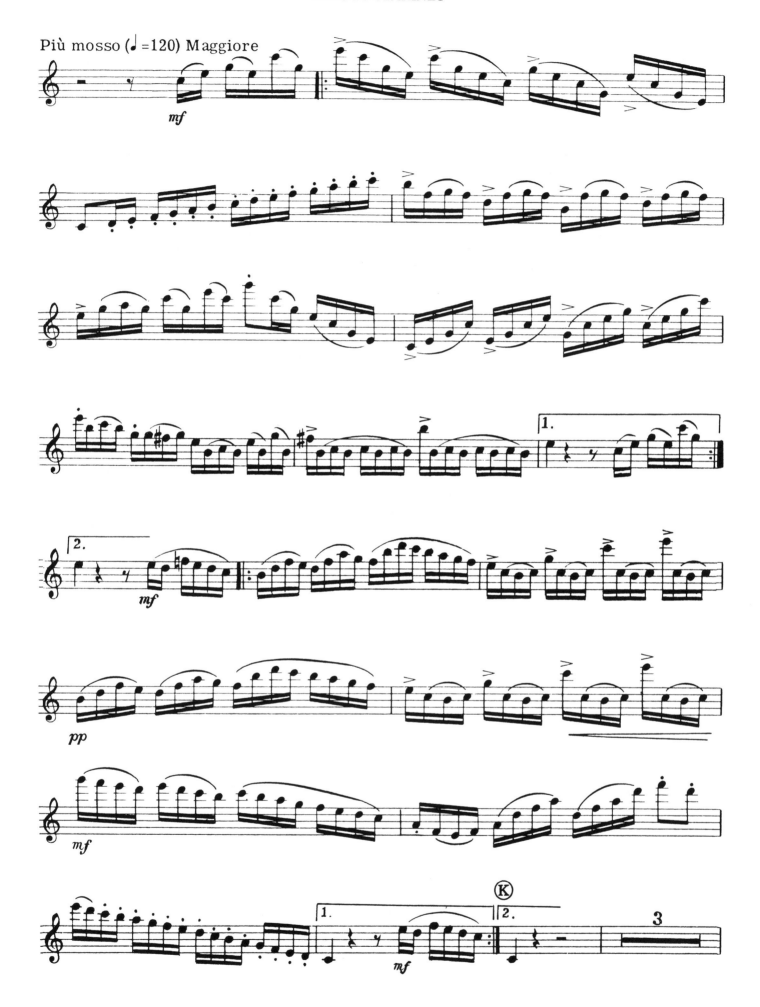

Più mosso (♩=120) Maggiore

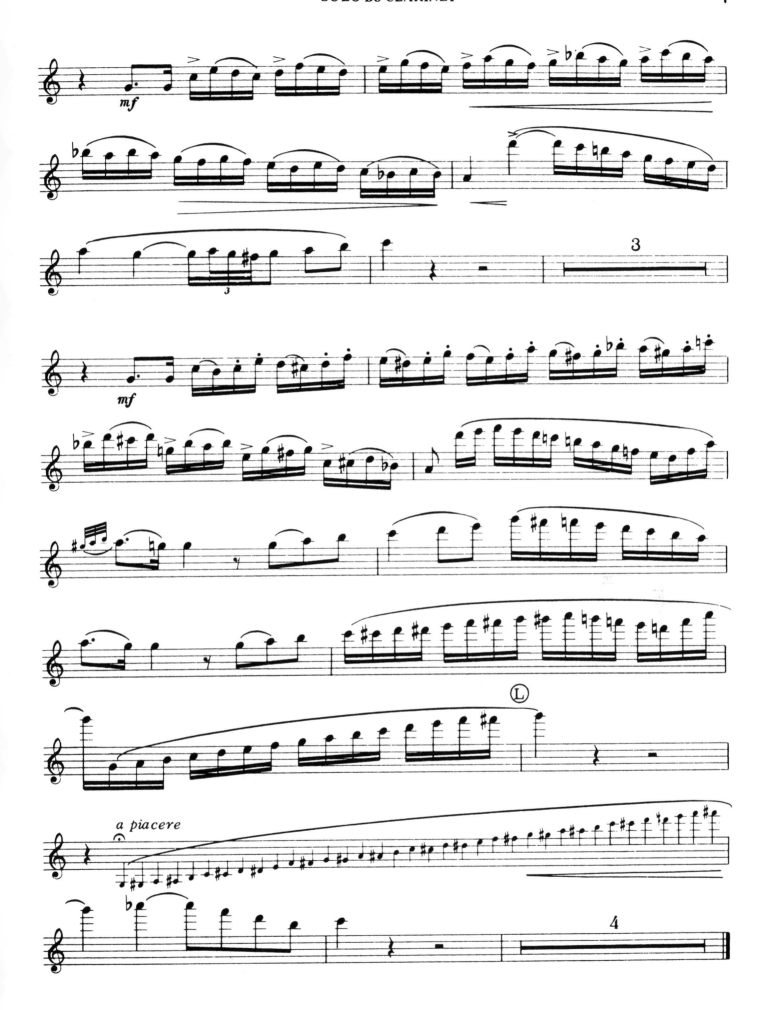

VAR. 3

18